Rookie
Read-About® Science

All About Light

D0474109

By Lisa Trumbauer

Consultants

David Larwa
National Science Consultant

Nanci R. Vargus, Ed.D.
Assistant Professor of Literacy
University of Indianapolis
Indianapolis, Indiana

Children's Press®
A Division of Scholastic Inc.
New York   Toronto   London   Auckland   Sydney
Mexico City   New Delhi   Hong Kong
Danbury, Connecticut

Designer: Herman Adler Design
Photo Researcher: Caroline Anderson
The photo on the cover shows an x-ray of a light bulb.

Library of Congress Cataloging-in-Publication Data

Trumbauer, Lisa, 1963–
  All about light / by Lisa Trumbauer.
      p. cm. — (Rookie read-about science)
Includes index.
Summary: An introduction to the sources and characteristics of light.
  ISBN 0-516-23446-3 (lib. bdg.)   0-516-25842-7 (pbk.)
  1. Light—Juvenile literature. [1. Light.] I. Title. II. Series.
  QC360.T78 2003
  535—dc22

                              2003019066

CHILDREN'S PRESS, and ROOKIE READ-ABOUT®,
and associated logos are trademarks and or registered trademarks
of Scholastic Library Publishing. SCHOLASTIC and associated logos
are trademarks and or registered trademarks of Scholastic Inc.

19 20 R 18 17

Scholastic Inc., 557 Broadway, New York, NY 10012.

What is light? Light is a
form of energy. Energy
makes things happen.

3

The sun gives off light.

Fire gives off light.

What happens when
the sun goes down?
It gets dark outside.

Long ago, people lit up
their homes with candles.

Today, people use electricity to light their homes. Electricity is another type of energy.

Light bulbs have wires in them. These wires glow when electricity runs through them.

Light moves very fast.

Turn on a lamp.

Right away, the room fills with light.

Light moves in a straight line.

Turn on a flashlight.

The beam of light is straight.

Light can bounce.

Shine a flashlight at
a mirror.

The beam of light bounces
off the mirror. It shines in
a different direction.

16

The moon looks bright at night. But the moon gives off no light of its own.

The moon is dark and
rocky. The sun's light
bounces off the moon.
This makes the moon
look bright.

When the moon is big and bright, we can see in the dark night.

Light can bend.

Put a straw in a glass of water. Now let the straw tip to the side.

What will happen?

The straw looks broken.

Light bends as it goes through water. The bending light makes the straw look broken.

Sunlight is made of many different colors of light.

Sunlight splits into these different colors when it passes through raindrops. This is how rainbows are made.

26

Light cannot go through everything. Shadows form when light is blocked.

Light makes shadows.
Light makes color.
Light makes things brighter.

Turn on the lights!

Words You Know

bounce

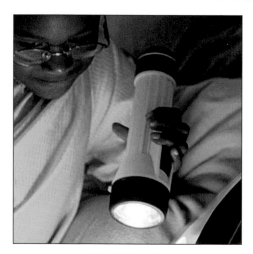

flashlight

light bulb

rainbow

shadows

31

Index

About the Author

Lisa Trumbauer has written a dozen books about the physical sciences and dozens more about other branches of science. She has also edited science programs for teachers of young children. Lisa lives in New Jersey with one dog, two cats, and her husband, Dave.

Photo Credits